big data lexicon

big data lexicon

No part of this publication may be reproduced, stored in a retrieval system or transmitted in any form or by any means, electronic, mechanical, photocopying, recording, scanning or otherwise, without prior written permission by the author. All trademarks and registered trademarks are the property of their respective owners. Nor author nor publisher share any association with any product or vendor mentioned.

Copyright © 2016-2019 Alexander Pericic. All rights reserved.

Pericic, Alexander.
  Over 200 Industry Terms Defined And Demystified With Easy To Understand Definitions / Alexander Pericic.
    p.   12.852 x 19.837 cm.
    ISBN-13: 978-1539360452
    ISBN-10: 1539360458
    1. Information management   2. Business and economics   I. Title

Printed in the United States of America

10 9 8 7 6 5 4

NEITSCH PRESS
P.O. Box 3262
Beverly Hills, CA 90212
www.neitsch-group.com

LIMIT OF LIABILITY
DISCLAIMER OF WARRANTY

THE PUBLISHER AND THE AUTHOR MAKE NO REPRESENTATIONS OR WARRANTIES WITH RESPECT TO THE ACCURACY OR COMPLETENESS OF THE CONTENTS OF THIS WORK AND SPECIFICALLY DISCLAIM ALL WARRANTIES, INCLUDING WITHOUT LIMITATION WARRANTIES OF FITNESS FOR A PARTICULAR PURPOSE. NO WARRANTY MAY BE CREATED OR EXTENDED BY SALES OR PROMOTIONAL MATERIALS. THE ADVICE AND STRATEGIES CONTAINED HEREIN MAY NOT BE SUITABLE FOR EVERY SITUATION. THIS WORK IS SOLD WITH THE UNDERSTINDING THAT THE PUBLISHER IS NOT ENGAGED IN RENDERING LEGAL, ACCOUNTING, OR OTHER PROFESSIONAL SERVICES. IF PROFESSIONAL ASSISTANCE IS REQUIRED, THE SERVICES OF A COMPETENT AND/OR LICENSED PROFESSIONAL SHOULD BE SOUGHT. NEITHER THE PUBLISHER NOR THE AUTHOR SHALL BE LIABLE FOR ANY DAMAGES ARISING HEREFROM. THE FACT THAT A STRATEGY, ORGANIZATION OR WEBSITE IS REFERRED TO IN THIS WORK AS A CITATION AND/OR A POTENTIAL SOURCE OF FURTHER INFORMATION DOES NOT MEAN THAT THE AUTHOR OR THE PUBLISHER ENDORSES THE INFORMATION THE ORGANIZATION OR WEBSITE OR ANY RECOMMENDATIONS IT MAY MAKE. FURTHER, READERS HOULD BE AWARE THAT INTERNET WEBSITES LISTED IN THIS WORK MAY HAVE CHANGED OR DISAPPEARED BETWEEN WHEN THIS WORK WAS WRITTEN AND THE PRESENT. SCENARIOS AND EXAMPLES ARE FICTIONAL AND ANY RESEMBLANCE TO ANY REAL WORK OR STRATEGY WITHOUT AN EXPLICIT REFERENCE IS PURELY COINCIDENTAL.

contents

A 1

B 5

C 9

D 15

E 25

F 27

G 29

H 31

I 35

J 39

K 41

L	43
M	45
N	49
O	51
P	53
Q	57
R	59
S	63
T	69
U	71
V	73
W	75
X	77
Z	79

author

ALEXANDER PERICIC NEITSCH, MSEE, PRINCE2, ITIL is an international advisor and consultant focused on emerging technologies, big data analytics, software development, visual design, and management strategy for business, solving longstanding, *unsolvable* problems.

His work has taken him across the globe, inside a multitude of leading organizations, bringing innovation and streamlining operations across the world in nearly 200 countries.

Alexander holds M.S. and B.S. degrees in Electrical Engineering from Clarkson University and is based in Los Angeles and New York.

foreword

WHAT YOU HOLD IN YOUR HAND is a concise, straightforward, excellent primer on big data analytics. Which is to say that this book is a vast amount of potential energy. Which is to say money and knowledge.

Your enterprise has likely collected much data, as one might gather paints, an easel, and canvas. Few do much with these tools that future generations will care about. Alexander explains the basics of blending colors, brush strokes, and shadowing, so you can create your Mona Lisa; your perfectly efficient running machine, your best quarter yet.

Many applied mathematicians, like myself, with experience in data analytics, could write a technical introduction to big data. But it takes Alexander's extensive experience with the corporate world to so perfectly blend the vernacular and mindset of the business world with the technical aspects of putting your data to work for you.

—DR. JESSE STONE, PH.D

preface

WITHOUT MUCH ADO, I present to you in no small part, a comprehensive big data lexicon. I've defined over 200 terms for your easy reference, whenever, wherever.

You will notice I intentionally strive to keep the definitions brief and as close to one line as possible, to facilitate conversations at all levels.

—ALEXANDER PERICIC, M.S.E.E.

In omnibus requiem quaesivi,
et nusquam inveni nisi in angulo cum libro.

—THOMAS À KEMPIS

Abstraction
Taking a higher level view, usually done for simplification purposes.

Alpha
Part of the SDLC, the alpha phase is the first phase of functional software testing. Software in this phase is usually given a version number followed by the letter 'a' or the word 'alpha'.

ACID
Acronym for Atomicity, Consistency, Isolation, and Durability, used to categorize database software and its transactions for operational reliability. For example, you'd want your financial software to be ACID-compliant.

Adicity
See Arity.

Agile
A set of principles for rapid software development where an incremental approach is used known as 'sprints', as an alternative to traditional project management methodologies and development is done in close communciation between developer and client where requirements can be changed in a more agile way. This does not mean that the change process does not exist, only that it is more accommodating than say, the *Waterfall* approach.

Aggregation
The process of collecting data from previous and current states. Commonly known as data aggregation.

AJAX
Acronym for Asynchronous JavaScript and XML, a client-side technology allowing background data operations to execute without interfering with the operation of the web page and DOM.

Algorithm
A set of steps or rules used to define an operational process of solving a particular problem or set of problems.

Anonymization
The process of removing personally-identifiable information (PII) from data sets.

AIDC
Acronym for Automatic identification and data capture defines the automatic method of identifying objects and collecting relevant data.

API
Acronym for Application Program Interface, APIs allow exchange of data between MVC components over a network.

Archiving
The process of moving older, or less-used data to another, usually slower and cheaper, data storage system.

Architecture
See *Solution architecture*.

Arity
Describes the number of arguments or operands that a function or command takes. In mathematics, this would be equivalent to *Rank*. Also called *adicity*, and *degree*.

Artificial Intelligence (AI)
A concept in the field of computer science wherein a computer, or machine exhibits independent rational thought similar to a biological, living being.

AsterixDB
Apache AsterixDB is an open source database management system for big data.

Atomicity
The first of the four properties of ACID, defining an indivisible and irreducible database operation wherein the operation is executed in its entirety, or not at all.

Aurora
Apache Aurora is a Mesos framework for automating long-duration services and cron jobs. *See Cron, Mesos*

Avro
Avro is a data serialization system which provides rich data structures, developed within Hadoop utilizing JSON for definitions and a compact binary format for serialization.

Behavioral analytics
Analysis of consumer behavior for new insights and predictions.

Beta
Part of the SDLC, the beta phase is the second phase of functional software testing. Software in this phase is usually given a version number followed by the letter 'b' or the word 'beta' and is a pre-cursor to RC software.

BigQuery
Google BigQuery is a serverless, fully managed, petabyte scale, low cost enterprise data warehouse for analytics.

Bigtable
Cloud Bigtable is Google's NoSQL big data database service.

Big Data
In its most-simplistic sense, it is all your data, combined and analyzed holistically for new insight–to help you make better decisions, faster.

Big Data Scientist
See Data Scientist.

Big Iron
See Mainframe.

Binary
A base-2 number system invented by Gottfriend Leibniz consisting of 0 and 1, in computers representing the ON or OFF state of a circuit. In computer programming, 8 bits of binary represent a *byte* and can have one of 256 values (i.e. $2^8 = 256$). Binary is evaluated from right to left, and each digit *n* represents a *bit* and has a value of 2^n depending on its placement, e.g. 01011000 is 88.
Also, referring to function of Arity 2. *See Arity.*

Biometrics
Measurable characteristics of an individual, such as one's fingerprint.

Bitemporal
Two or more alternate, independent timelines for data storage.

Bulk synchronous parallel (BSP)
A computing model for designing parallel algorithms, similar in purpose to PRAM.

Business Intelligence (BI)
Collection, analysis and conversion of data into information for enhanced insight into business through reports and visualizations.

C
Family of object-oriented programming languages, starting with the C programming language, invented by Dennis Ritchie.

C+
Short for ABCL/c+, it is an object-oriented, concurrent variant of ABCL/1 based on C rather than Lisp, and created by Akinori Yonezawa.

C++
A derivation of the C programming language designed by Bjarne Stroustrup, standardized in 1998.

C#
C-sharp is a C-family multi-paradigm, managed, type safe, object-oriented programming language, designed for the Common Language Infrastructure (CLI). Successor to C++ and C, the # symbol is a stylistic arrangement of four plus signs, sort of signifying an 2^n iteration of the language.

Cardinality
Describes the relationship of one data element to another (e.g., one-to-one, one-to-many, many-to-one, many-to-many).

Cartesian
Of, or relating to the Cartesian square, or Cartesian product, a mathematical concept named after René Descartes, where in analytical geometry the product of two sets $A \times B$ represents an n-tuple

Cascading
An application development platform for building data applications on Hadoop.

Cassandra
Apache Cassandra is a free, open-source, distributed database management system.

Chukwa
Apache Chukwa is an open source data collection system for monitoring large distributed systems, built on top of Hadoop Distributed File System (HDFS) and Map/Reduce framework.

Classification
The problem of classifying identified observations into categories, commonly related to fields of machine learning and statistics.

CLI
Acronym for Common Language Infrastructure, an open-specification developed by Microsoft that describes executable code and runtime enviroment for easy portability between computer platforms. For example, the .NET Framework.
Also, Command Line Interface.

Client-side
A set of operations performed in the client environment, this being the user's computer, most-commonly, as opposed to Server-side.

Clickstream
The stream of mouse clicks a user performs while navigating a website or using an application.

Cloud
The concept of cloud computing is using a network of remote servers for computing purposes.Similar to Mainframe computing (see Big Iron), but the computers are not physically collocated and are in the cloud.

Cluster
A group of machines performing a task or operation, such as a database cluster.

Clojure
A functional programming language with concise syntax, concurrency support and Java integration.

Cold storage
Retention of inactive, or dormant data on a long-term, low-cost basis. The data is not frequently used and takes some time to operationalize, but is available if needed.

Columnar database
A type of database management system which stores data in columns rather than rows. Advantages are reduced hard disk access times.

Comparative analysis
The process of determining logical conclusions from two or more data entities.

Comparator
A device used to compare a measurable dimension to an established reference.

Complex event processing (CEP)
Data processing of events that takes input of data from multiple sources, commonly used in deriving data-centric conclusions.

Confabulation
From Latin, *confabulari*–a questionable method of putting data together to support a decision after the fact.

Consistency
The second of the four properties of ACID, ensuring the database is always in a valid state.

Content management system (CMS)
A computer system specifically designed for easy publishing of content online to a web server or a web site. Usually equipped with a WYSIWYG editor.

Counter machine
An abstract register machine used in theoretical computer science to model computation in its most-primitive state.

Cron
A task-scheduling software utility for automatic execution of processes, or jobs on Unix-based operating systems.

Cross-channel analytics
Business analysis across several different channel to extract valuable intelligence for business.

Culturomics
A form of computational lexicology that studies human behavior and cultural trends through the quantitative analysis of digitized texts.

Dashboard
A one page (usually) visual overview of charts and tables drawn from key metrics of overall, or a specific area(s) of business.

Data aggregation
See Aggregation.

Data architecture
Architecture of data, its storage, its inputs and outputs, its including underlying rules and processes, and ultimate business goals.

Database
A system for storing data, usually made accessible to external systems and applications for storage and retrieval of data.

Database administrator (DBA)
Resource responsible for administering one or several databases, who understands the inner workings of the database systems, but also the structures of data.

Database as a service (DBaaS)
A database in the cloud, delivering similar functionality to traditional relational databases.

Database model
A model that shows the structure of a database. There are several database models based on varying concepts, most popular being (in alphabetical order): document, entity, hierarchical, network, object, relational and star. *See definitions below for each.*

DataOps
An automated, process-oriented approach to data analytics helping data scientist and data analyst teams to improve the quality of data and reduce cycle times.

Data center
A central repository of data storage systems—can be either virtual or physical.

Data cleansing
Also known as Data scrubbing, it is a process of maintaining database integrity through removing corrupt or incorrect data.

Data collection
The process of collecting data from a single or multiple sources.

Data custodian
A resource responsible for protecting data under the corporate data governance and security policies.

Data exhaust
Byproduct of normal use of modern computer applications that collect and store data often times necessary for their operation, such as cache files, cookies, and other temporary files.

Data feed
A stream of data usually in XML or JSON format served by a web service based on input parameters of the request. For example, live weather updates or news for a particular ZIP code.

Data governance
Corporate set of rules and policies that describe formal management of organizational data assets.

Data integration
Selective combination of data from two or more sources to obtain intelligence for a specific business purpose.

Data integrity
Accuracy and consistency of data.

Database management system (DBMS)
A system program, or application that is responsible for managing databases.

Data mart
A smaller subset of the Data warehouse, specifically chosen for operations of a particular business unit, or department.

Data migration
The process of copying data from one place to another. For example, copying data to a newer, faster server.

Data mining
Skilled examination of various data sets to find new intelligence and reveal new relationships.

Data model(ing)
An abstract model showing relationships of real world components represented by data, and their inherent data flow. *See Database model.*

Data point
A single, discrete instance of recorded data.

Data profiling
The process of collecting statistical summaries about a particular set or sets of data.

Data quality
A measure of quality of data based on its accuracy and relevance.

Data replication
A process of replicating data from a primary system where the data originated to another system.

Data repository
Usually centralized storage where data is permanently stored.

Data science
The study of data to extract meaningful intelligence for a business purpose.

Data scientist
An interdisciplinary resource skilled to extract intelligence from data using numerical analysis or statistical methods combined with expertise in computer science, such as programming, or database administration.

Data set
Data, usually of a certain theme, collected together in a database, an archive file, or set of files, ready to be processed or transferred.

Data source
The origin of a set, or multiple sets of data.

Data steward
A resource responsible for management of data elements, including their metadata.

Data structure
An organization of data for a specific use or purpose.

Data visualization
A visual representation of (usually) structured data, such as data tables, through charts and graphs. See Dashboard.

Data warehouse (DW)
The central repository of all organizational data.

De-identification
See Anonymization.

Deep Blue
An IBM artificial intelligence computer and chess-playing champion.

Deep Thunder
An IBM research program aimed to improve short-term weather forecasting, touted as the World's Most Advanced Hyper-Local Weather Forecasting Model for Businesses.

Degree
See Arity.

DevOps
A software development methodology designed to improve quality and alignment to business objectives while shortening the SDLC by combining IT and software development in a cohesive manner.

Disaster recovery (DR)
A set of procedures for restoring a database from disaster, and mitigating any data loss.

Distributed cache
Secondary, fast-access memory cache distributed on several servers for scalability and transactional capacity.

Distributed file system
A system of allocating files across multiple servers. See HDFS.

Distributed object
One of a set of objects distributed throughout different memory spaces and/or multiple systems.

Distributed processing
Sharing of a processing load by several interconnected systems to improve performane and reduce load on each single one.

Document management system (DMS)
A computer system specifically designed for managing documents in electronic format, and frequently includes versioning control, and workflows.

Document-oriented database
A computer system specifically designed for managing document-oriented information or semi-structured data. See NoSQL.

DOM
Acronym for Document Object Model, a cross-platform, language-independent API that interprets HTML, XHTML and XML documents most-often in a visual manner such as a web browser.

Drill
Apache Drill is an open source, low-latency query engine for big data that delivers secure and interactive SQL analytics at petabyte scale.

Durability

The last of the four properties of ACID, ensuring that committed transactions remain committed permanently.

Elasticsearch
An open-source search engine based on Apache Lucene, providing distributed, multitenant-capable full-text search.

Enterprise data warehouse (EDW)
See Data warehouse

Exabyte (EB)
A unit of information equal to one billion gigabytes.

Exploratory analysis
A 'free-verse exploration' of one or more data sets to reveal meaningful characteristics, content and relationships.

External data
Data not contained within a particular system, but rather is external to it. Data from an outside source.

Extract, transform, and load (ETL)
Three separate functions usually programmed in succession to extract data from one system, transform it, and load it into another system.

Failover

A method of redundancy to maintaing operation by automatically switching to another system when a failure event has occurred in the main system.

Flume

Apache Flume lets Hadoop users ingest high-volume streaming data into HDFS for storage.

Fortran

The oldest high-level programming language still in use today, originally developed by IBM in 1957. The name comes from the words Formula Translation.

Gartner
A trusted research and advisory source providing insight into the information technology and other fields. See Magic Quadrant (MQ).

GeoJSON
An open-standard data-interchange format based on JSON featuring geographical features along with non-spatial attributes.

Graph
A type of data structure wherein a finite set of vertices and nodes describe relationships between a set of elements in either a directed, or undirected graph.

Graph database
A type of database used for storing and querying of graphs.

Grid computing

Mutual sharing of computer resources by several computers across a network.

Hadoop
Part of the Apache project, Hadoop is an open-source programming framework based on Java for efficient processing and storage of big data structures across a distributed computing environment.

Hama
Apache Hama is a framework for big data analytics utilizing the Bulk Synchronous Parallel (BSP) computing model.

HANA
SAP HANA is an in-memory, column-oriented relational database management system.

HAWQ
Apache Hadoop native instance of SQL utilizing convenience of Hadoop and advantages of an MPP database.

HBase
Apache HBase is an open-source Hadoop database that is a scalable and distributed big data store.

HCatalog
A table and storage management layer for Hadoop, supporting Pig, MapReduce and others.

HDFS (Hadoop Distributed File System)
HDFS (Hadoop Distributed File System) the storage layer of Hadoop, is a distributed, scalable, Java-based file system adept at storing large volumes of unstructured.

Helix
Apache Helix is an automated cluster management framework for disaster recovery and resource reconfiguration.

High availability (HA)
A measure of reliability, wherein a system or component is continuously operational, approaching 100% uptime.

Hive
Apache Hive is a SQL-like, database query interface to Apache Hadoop

Hortonworks
A software company behind the development and support of Apache Hadoop.

HTTP
The main protocol used by the World Wide Web (WWW) defining how bits of information, or messages, are transmitted between servers. *See HTTP Server.*

HTTP Server
A computer host and underlying software to transmit and receive HTTP-protocol requests, generally running on port 80. When you visit a web site, an HTTP Server is serving you content.

The main protocol used by the World Wide Web (WWW) defining how bits of information, or messages, are transmitted between servers. *See HTTP Server*

Hue
Acronym for Hadoop User Experience, Hue is an open source Web interface for analyzing data with Apache Hadoop.

IATI
Acronym for International Aid Transparency Initiative, IATI is a voluntary, multi-stakeholder initiative that seeks to improve the transparency of aid, development, and humanitarian resources in order to increase their effectiveness.

IATI Standard
A format and framework for publishing data under the IATI on development cooperation activities. Organisations implement IATI by publishing their aid information in IATI's agreed electronic format (XML).

Impala
Cloudera Impala is an open-source massively parralel processing (MPP) SQL-query engine for Apache Hadoop.

In-database analytics
An enterprise data warehouse (EDW) system combined with an analytics database platform for better parallel processing, partitioning, scalability and optimization, in particular for maximizing analytical capabilities.

Inferencing
Using historic and present state data to draw inferences about a possible future state, with some level of calculated certainty.

IA
Acronym for Information Architecture, the design and structure of information within an environment, such as web application or web site.

In-memory database (IMDB)
A database system that relies on system memory for primary data storage.

In-memory data grid (IMDG)
A data structure which resides entirely in system memory and may be distributed.

Internet of Things (IoT)
The networking of 'things': connected devices and smart devices that collect and exchange data across a network.

Isolation

The third of the four properties of ACID, ensuring that concurrent transaction execution produces the same result as as serial transaction execution.

ITIL

Acronym (fmr.) for Information Technology Infrastructure Library, a set of best practices for ITSM, originally developed in the 1980s by the UK Government's Central Computer and Telecommunications Agency (CCTA).

ITSM

Acronym for Information Technology Service Management.

Java
An object-oriented programming language designed by James Gosling.

JavaScript
An object-oriented programming language, primarily used in web page development alongside HTML and CSS.

jQuery
A cross-platform JavaScript library facilitating advanced JavaScript operations, mostly in web page development.

JRE
Acronym for Java Runtime Environment, a Java virtual machine, core classes and libraries to allow development and running of Java applications.

JSON
Acronym for JavaScript Object Notation, JSON is an easy to read, easy to parse data-interchange format.

JVM
Acronym for Java Virtual Machine, a runtime environment that enables a machine to run a Java application.

Kafka

Apache Kafka is a distributed streaming platform used for building real-time streaming data pipelines and applications.

Key-value pair (KVP)

A set of two linked data items, frequently used in lookup tables.

Key-value store

A type of database used to store key-value pairs.

LAMP
Acronym for Linux operating system, Apache web server, MySQL RDBMS, and PHP programming language, as the four original building blocks of a LAMP web service solution stack.

Latency
A measure of delay between stimulation and response, usually measured in nanoseconds (ns) for memory.

Linked data
Data connected together through meaningful relationships to facilitate querying.

Lisp
The second-oldest high-level programming language, originally standardized in 1958. *Also see Fortran.*

Load balancing
Distributing processing workload in a balanced way across several machines to increase reliability and capacity.

Location analytics
Analysis of data sets along their geospatial coordinates.

Location data
Geospatial data—latitude, longitude, elevation, frequently recorded by a GPS unit.

Log file
An electronic file usually in Text-format which contains rows of event data organized by time.

Machine-generated data
Data automatically generated by computer software without a human input.

Machine learning
A derivative of pattern recognition and computational learning theory in artificial intelligence, wherein machines are able to 'learn' without explicit programming.

Magic Quadrant (MQ)
Brand name of Gartner for its series of research and market reports providing qualitative analyses on select markets.

Mahout
Apache Mahout is an open-source environment for quickly creating scalable preformant machine learning applications.

Mainframe
Large, high-performance computer system used for mission-critical, large-scale computing operations and applications requiring more processing power and reliability a smaller, or personal computer can provide.

Main-memory database (MMDB)
See In-memory database (IMDB).

Many-to-many
See Cardinality.

Many-to-one
See Cardinality.

MapReduce
A method of big data processing wherein a large job is split into small chunks that are then processed by a map operation in parallel. The outputs are then handled by a reduce operation to tie in the results.

MarkLogic
An enterprise, schema-agnostic NoSQL database designed to run on-premises or in the cloud.

Mashup
A combination of various data sources or elements to produce a cohesive output.

Massively parallel processing (MPP)
Coordinated, loosely coupled processing by a large number of processors.

Mesos
Apache Mesos is an open-source software framework used to manage computer clusters.

Message
Unit of information that is exchanged between server and client. It can be formatted in any number of ways to coform to some protocol, for example an HTTP request.

Metadata
Data describing other data, usually to improve searchability. For example, an XML file with information about a MP4 video file.

Middleware
Software running on an operating system, facilitating the operation of a higher-level program by providing relevant services.

MongoDB
An open-source NoSQL document database.

MPP database
A database optimized for parallel processing.

Multi-dimensional database (MDB)
A database optimized for data warehouse and online analytical processing (OLAP).

Multivariate database
A type of NoSQL, multi-dimensional database.

MVC
Acronym for Model-View-Controller, a software architecture wherein an application is divided in those three parts.

MySQL
An open-source, SQL-based RDBMS. Also, central component of LAMP.

NAS
Acronym for Network Attached Storage, a file storage server attached to a network.

.NET
.NET or .NET Framework is a CLI software programming framework developed by Microsoft.

Network analysis
Mathematical analysis of the network of entities and their complex relationships.

NewSQL
A buzzword naming the newest range of scalable SQL and NoSQL databases, coined by Matthew Aslett of 451 Group.

Node
A single machine in a cluster of distributed machines.

Node.js
An open-source, Server-side JavaScript runtime environment.

NoSQL
Acronym for Not-only-SQL, describing database systems that store data using a variety of database models beyond the relational model.

NULL
A special marker used in Structured Query Language (SQL) to indicate or logically confirm that data is empty, undefined, is of, or has, no value.

Nullary
Referring to function of Arity 0. *See Arity.*

Object database
A type of database wherein information is represented in the form of objects.

One-to-many
See Cardinality.

One-to-one
See Cardinality.

Online analytical processing (OLAP)
Multi-dimensional analysis of business data for complex data modeling, optimized for read-only operation.

Online transactional processing (OLTP)
A type of system which handles transaction-oriented applications, in contrast to OLAP supports read, insert, update and delete operations.

Ontology
The definition of relationships within a taxonomy.

Oozie
Apache Oozie is a workflow scheduler system for management of Hadoop jobs.

OpenDremel
Integrated with Apache Drill, OpenDremel is an open-source version of Google's Big Query.

OpenNLP
Apache OpenNLP is a machine learning toolkit for natural language processing. *See NLP.*

Open Data Center Alliance (ODCA)
An independent organiation for shaping the future of cloud computing.

Operational data store (ODS)
A database containing select, operational data that is frequently needed, and available in real-time, or near-real-time.

Parallel algorithm
The opposite of a serial algorithm, a parallel algorithm can be executed in chunks across many systems, and its results combined together for the final aggregate result.

Parallel processing
See Parallel algorithm.

Parallel random access machine (PRAM)
A shared-memory abstract machine as the parallel-computing analogy to the random-access machine (RAM).

Pattern recognition
The process of classification of input data based on pre-defined rules and categories.

Pentaho
An open-source suite of Business Intelligence products offering big data capabilities.

Periscope
A software package offering visualizations of SQL-queries.

Personally Identifiable Information
See PII.

Petabyte (PB)
One million gigabytes.

PHP)
Acronym for Hypertext Preprocessor, a server-side scripting language designed for web development.

Pig
Apache Pig is a platform for analyzing large data sets utilizing a language called Pig Latin.

Pig Latin
A language used in Apache Pig, which abstracts the programming in a similar way SQL does.

PII
Acronym for Personally Identifiable Information. Relates to pieces of data that could be used to distinguish between persons and potentially reveal the identity of a private person.

Predictive analytics
A data mining branch wherein past and present states are mined for development of a predictive model which can then predict the future state of a variable.

Predictive modeling
See Predictive analytics.

Pruning
The process of removing older, less-active data from an active operational database to an archival medium to optimaze performance.

Public data
Public information or data sets freely available to the public.

QBE
Acronym for Query By Example, a user-friendly method of querying a database wherein only simple parameters need be entered, and the task of building a complete query with correct syntax is up to the software.

QR Code
An acronym for Quick Response Code, is square matrix of dots, similar to a barcode found on product packaging, it encodes specific information such as perhaps a web site address.

Quaternary
Referring to function of Arity 4. *See Arity.*

Query
A request for information from a database.

Queue

A stream, or line of entities arranged serially en route to a process. For example, a queue of documents waiting to be printed, one after another.

R
A language and environment for statistical computing and graphics.

Random access machine (RAM)
An abstract machine identical to a multi-register counter machine but with added indirect addressing, frequently used for computational complexity analysis.

RBM
Acronym for Results Based Management, a management strategy which maps business outcome contributions and utilizes a feedback loop concept to fulfill strategic goals.

RC
Acronym for Release Candidate, it refers to beta software being developed under the SDLC process. Software in this phase is usually complete and functional enough for general release unless failures occur during testing.

RDBMS
Acronym for Relational Database Management System.

RDF
Acronym for Resource Description Framework, a model for data interchange structured in the form of subject-predicate-object (SPO) expressions.

Real-time data (RTD)
Data processed and delivered nearly immediately after collection with no, or minimal delay.

Re-identification
The process of attaching Personally Identifiable Information (PII) to anonymized data.

REST
Acronym for Representational State Transfer, wherein each unique URL or endpoint is a representation of some object.

Runtime

Also called *Runtime system*, or *Runtime environment*, a computer enviroment (i.e. a system environment of software libraries, variables, constants) created to support the running of a software program, also called the execution of a program (e.g. Windows Runtime or WinRT).

SAML
Acronym for Security Assertion Markup Language, a framework for structuring authentication information in an XML format.

SAN
Acronym for Storage Area Network, typically a high-speed array of network-connected storage systems, commonly referred to as a SAN Drive.

Scalability
Ability of a system to maintain same level of performance as demands grow, either by adding more memory, more processors, or even more distributed machines.

Schema
A definition of a data storage structure—a file, a database, a system.

Scrum
An agile software development model wherein a number of small teams incrementally and iteratively build a deliverable.

SDLC
Acronym for Software Development Life Cycle, a process describing all aspects of development of a particular software product.

Semantics, Semantic search
A method of producing highly-relevant search results through analysis of the science of meaning in language usually found in relationships. *See RDF.*

Semi-structured data
Data which does not conform to a formal structure but still contains defined hierarchical structure.

Server-side
A set of operations performed in the server environment, as opposed to Client-side.

Service catalog
A listing of services offered, usually by an in-house IT department to other business units.

Service management
A set of practices ensuring quality of service and alignment to business goals is maintained across services offered.

Sharding
Taking a very large (slow) database and splitting it into smaller, faster, more responsive managed data structures, or shards.

Silo
An isolated, disparate system.

SLA
An acronym for Service Level Agreement, an agreement between you and a service provider offering certain levels of service, such as '99% uptime guarantee'.

SOAP
Acronym for Simple Object Access Protocol, SOAP exchanges structured information through web services over networks.

Spatial analysis
See Location analysis.

SQL
Acronym for Structured Query Language, SQL is special programming language for manipulating data and functions of a SQL database.

SQL Server
Microsoft SQL Server is an RDBMS and the de facto standard in relational databases with structured data.

SQL Server Express
Free, scaled-down version of Microsoft SQL Server.

Sqoop
Apache Sqoop is a bulk data transfer tool for use between Apache Hadoop and structured databases.

SSAS
Acronym for SQL Server Analysis Services, an OLAP tool used for analysis of information across multiple data sources.

SSIS
Acronym for SQL Server Integration Services, an ETL tool for SQL Server offering data integration and workflow features.

SSRS
Acronym for SQL Server Reporting Services, a web application reporting system included with SQL Server services.

Solution architecture (SA)
The structure of a system of a specific solution delivered to meet business goals.

Storage
A system or method of permanently storing data.f

Storm
Apache Storm is an open-source distributed real-time computation system.

Software as a service (SaaS)
A licensing and delivery model where software is licensed on a subscription basis.

Structured data
Data organized according to a schema, a well-defined structure, such as rows and columns.

Symmetrically parallel system (SMP)
Coordinated, tightly coupled processing by a number of processors that share a common operating system and an I/O bus.

Syntactical
Of, or referring to *syntax*. *See Syntax.*

Syntax
The proper writing of a command function also with regard to its arity. *See Arity.*

Taxonomy
A naming or classification system.

Ternary
Referring to function of Arity 3. *See Arity.*

Text mining
The process of analyzing text for high-quality information.

Thrift
Apache Thrift is a data-type definition language and binary communication protocol.

Transactional data
Data recorded from a single event of information exchange within a single process, or transation.

Triple

A data entity composed of a subject-predicate-object structure. *See RDF.*

Triple store

A database for storage and querying of triples.

Unary
Referring to function of Arity 1. *See Arity.*

Unstructured data
Data that has no identifiable structure, such as the body of an e-mail message, or freeform text.

UX
An acronym for User Experience, which describes an end customer's interaction with a particular product.

Variety
The number of types of data.

Velocity
The speed of data flow, and processing.

Veracity
The accuracy, relevance and quality of data.

Virtual, Virtualization
Abstracting a physical system into a virtual environment, such as running a PC environment inside a Mac system by way of a software system emulator.

Volume
The amount of data.

Vs, the four
The four Vs describing big data: Volume, Velocity, Variety, Veracity.

Waterfall model
A software development process wherein development flows like a waterfall from Requirements, Design, Implementation, Verification and finally, Maintenance. Contemporary approach to development, now more often replaced by the *agile* methodology. *See Agile.*

WCF
Acronym for Windows Communication Foundation, WCF is a framework for creating service-oriented applications and data-interchange between endpoints over networks.

Web service
A data-interchange facility using a structured approach to transmit data over networks.

WinRT
Short for Windows Runtime. *See Runtime.*

Woden
Apache Woden is a sub-project of Apache Web Services projects used for creating WSDL documents.

Workflow
A systematically defined sequential process with each component assigned to a particular person, persons or business unit to fulfill a deliverable.

WSDL
A definition of a web service endpoint in an XML format.

WYSIWYG
Acronym for *What You See Is What You Get*, it commonly refers to an electronic copy editor, wherein what you type on the screen is what will be produced in the output, either as a web page, or a printed document.

XML
Acronym for eXtensible Markup Language, XML is an easy to read, easy to parse data-interchange format.

XML Database
A type of database that stores information in an XML format.

XSD
An acronym for XML Schema Definition, a document with file extension .XSD describing the schema of an XML document.

XSLT
An acronym for eXtensible Stylesheet Language Transformations, a language for manipulating the structure of XML documents programmaticaly.

XQuery

A query and functional programming languages frequently used with XML and JSON formats.

Zettabyte (ZB)
A unit of information equal to one sextillion bytes.

ZooKeeper
Apache Zookeper is an open-source, distributed, hierarchical key-value store that provides operational services for a Hadoop cluster.

thanks

I would like to acknowledge all the kind and talented individuals who have made this work possible and to extend a special thanks to a select few of my past and present engagements and clients, in no particular order:

2013 Nobel Peace Prize Laureate The Organisation for the Prohibition of Chemical Weapons (OPCW), the United Nations and United Nations Development Programme (UNDP), Netherlands Organisation for Applied Scientific Research (TNO), MarkLogic Corporation, Calpine Corporation, The Walt Disney Company and General Networks.

And of course, to my family.

consulting

For consulting or advisory services, or speaking engagements, you may write to the Publisher at neitsch@gmx.com.

errata

For errors or omissions, or to request addition of specific terms to be defined in the next edition, you may write to the Publisher at `neitsch@gmx.com`.

www.ingramcontent.com/pod-product-compliance
Lightning Source LLC
Chambersburg PA
CBHW070327190526
45169CB00005B/1779